About the author.

The author is a retired physics teacher who hopes that Golfing Teddy will encourage young children to take an interest in the amazing world around them.

This book is about the life story of the frog told with pictures and a follow up story of The Frog Prince to show that kindness to all creatures is a good virtue.

Other books

The Story of Yorkshire Ted. A Golfing Bear

published by New Generation Publishing

Golfing Teddy and The Frog Prince

This little book is dedicated to all children who love teddy bears and golf.

Thank you Hollie Nevison and Sue Porter for your drawings.

Golfing Teddy is a golf mascot. He makes friends with a toy frog and together they learn about real frogs and their life story in words and pictures.

Ted tells his friends the story of The Frog Prince.

Another Adventure for Yorkshire Ted.

Once upon a time a toy maker made a lovely little teddy bear. He gave him a bright shiny golf club and a special golfing hat.

Little Ted was looking forward to becoming a present for a boy or girl who would take him to play golf.

The toy maker put Ted into a parcel to send him to the toy shop.

The labels got muddled up and Ted went to a china shop instead.

He sat with the cups and saucers and he was very sad. Who would now take him to play golf?

Lucky Ted was rescued by a kind lady. He now lives with Aunt Heather.

He has a bedroom of his own and lots of toys to play with.

He also likes to play in the garden with the other toys and he loves to climb trees.

In the garden there is a pond and one day Ted met a toy frog sitting there. The frog looked unhappy.

'Why are you so sad'? said Ted.

The frog replied, 'There are no little frogs in this pond. I am all on my own. I have no friends.'

'I will be your friend' said Ted 'And I will call you Freddie Frog.'

So they sat by the pond and talked.

Sometimes they called, 'Hello' to the goldfish.

Suddenly Freddie said, 'What is that stick you are holding in your hand'?

'Silly Freddie' answered Ted, 'That stick is a golf club. I am the mascot of a team of girl golfers.

I carry my golf club everywhere in case they need me to come quickly and bring them luck.'

'I am a very good mascot' said Ted.

'You are lucky to have a lot of friends' replied Freddie.

Just then Ted had a bright idea. 'I will ask Aunt Heather if she can get some little frogs for you to play with.'

'Oh, thank you,' answered the frog.

Aunt Heather explained that in the spring time mother frogs, with the help from father frogs, lay eggs in the pond.

These eggs are called frog spawn.

After a few weeks these eggs grow into tadpoles and then finally into little frogs.

The next day Aunt Heather and Ted went to the village pond to see if there was some frog spawn.

Ted was excited to see a lot of frog spawn so they brought a jar full of eggs and put them into Freddie's pond.

Aunt Heather said that the little black dot in the middle will grow and get longer and develop into a tadpole.

The tadpole eats the jelly to escape into the pond and swim around.

Ted and Freddie had to wait about three weeks for the tadpoles to emerge.

The big day finally came. Ted and Freddie saw the first little tadpoles swimming in the small pond.

'They are very tiny' said Freddie.

Tadpoles have a long tail and they use this tail to move around. They wiggle it to swim.

For little creatures they move very quickly.

Ted and Freddie saw lots of little tadpoles.

They liked to hide under the leaves in the pond.

Tadpoles are usually shiny black but some are brown and furry.

Aunt Heather put some of the tadpoles in a glass jar so it was easier to watch them grow.

Sometimes Aunt Heather cooked lettuce for them. They loved that!

They also liked to eat pink fish food.

Ted and Freddie watched the tadpoles grow bigger and bigger.

Tadpoles have a long tail when they are young but then they they start to grow two little legs at the back of the body.

After a few more weeks two little legs grow at the front of the body.

The body changes shape.

These nearly frogs are called froglets.

When the legs get stronger the tail disappears and the little creature can now jump.

They need to practise jumping in and out of the pond.

Soon they are strong enough to live outside the pond because they are now frogs!

'Oh, look' said Ted 'A tiny frog.

Now Freddie has frogs to play with. Freddie said 'Thank you very much Ted'.

Suddenly Ted remembered he knew a story about a special frog. 'Shall I tell you'? he asked?

'Yes, please', replied Freddie.

Ted sat in his pretend boat and told all the toys and the pond animals the story of The Frog Prince.

Once upon a time there was a handsome prince who lived in a large palace.

He was very happy until a spiteful fairy turned him into a frog. He had to live in a pond instead of a nice palace.

One day a little princess was playing by the pond and her beautiful golden ball fell into the pond with a SPLASH and disappeared.

She cried so much that a frog jumped out of the pond to see what was wrong.

The princess stopped crying and looked at the frog for a few minutes and saw that he was wearing a crown.

She was very cheeky and said to the frog, 'Why are you wearing a crown Mr Frog'?

Mr Frog replied 'I have a secret so I cannot tell you why'.

The frog told her, 'l will find your ball and bring it to you if you let me come and live with you in the palace'.

The princess wanted her golden ball so badly. So she promised the frog that he could come and live with her if he found her ball.

The frog jumped in and found the golden ball.

The naughty princess did not want the cold, wet frog to live with her so she took the ball and ran home.

That night the king, the queen and the princess were having supper when there was a knock on the door.

Rat-a tat-tat!

The door was opened and there stood the frog.

The frog told the king that the princess had broken her promise to let him live with her.

The king was not pleased with the princess and told her that promises must always be kept.

He invited the frog to join them for supper.

The frog sat at the table next to the princess and ate from her plate.

When the frog was tired she had to take him to her bedroom and put him on the end of her bed to sleep.

In the morning the princess woke up to find that the frog had disappeared.

The frog came back the next night and stayed with the princess but disappeared in the morning.

But on the third night the princess had a very big shock because the frog turned into a handsome prince.

The princess had broken the wicked fairy's spell by being kind to the frog.

The king said that the new prince could stay in the palace and play with the princess.

The king and the queen said that when the prince and princess were older they could marry and live happily ever after.

Freddie Frog and the pond animals loved the story of The Frog Prince and asked Ted to tell them another story.

Ted told them that he was rather tired but another day he would tell them about the stars and the Moon and especially the Story of The Men who went to the Moon.

www.ingramcontent.com/pod-product-compliance
Lightning Source LLC
Chambersburg PA
CBHW050921290526
45792CB00002B/847